A Fine Grammar of Bones

A Fine Grammar of Bones

Méira Cook

Turnstone Press

Turnstone Press
607-100 Arthur Street
Winnipeg, Manitoba
Canada R3B 1H3

Turnstone Press gratefully acknowledges the assistance
of the Canada Council and the Manitoba Arts Council.

Cover illustration: Jeff Funnell

Cover design: Doowah Design

Text design: Manuela Dias

This book was printed and bound in Canada by
Hignell Printing for Turnstone Press.

Canadian Cataloguing in Publication Data

Cook, Méira, 1964-

A fine grammar of bones

Poems.
ISBN 0-88801-171-7

I. Title.

PS8555.064F5 1993   C811'.54   C93-098060-3
PR9199.3.C66F5 1993

for Mark

Acknowledgements

Thank you to Don Coles and Dennis Cooley whose reading of these poems was invaluable and to Katharine Bitney, Di Brandt, Laurie Lam and Carol Shields for their advice.
I am grateful for the support of the Manitoba Arts Council and the Banff School of the Arts.

Some of these pieces have appeared in *Absinthe, Border Crossings, Canadian Fiction Magazine, Grain* and *Prairie Fire.*

Contents

The Crazy Woman Poems

crazyWoman   3
the earth my body this tree   4
with words my tentpegs   5
fat lady suites   7
crazyWoman loses a button   8
a fine grammar of bones   11
burning bush   12
a short growing season   13
crazyWoman remembers water   14

Palm of the Hand Stories

The schoolteacher his wife their dog
    and the chicken   19
My mother's heart My mother's bitter heart   21
Take one of mine said Olivia   25
Something I've been meaning   28
A little bird dreamed Maya   31
Anyplace but here   34

Tailored Desires

girl in a yellow dress   39
a taste for butter   41
redDress   44

This Time of Year

    these thirsty flowers   49

    i mean coyotes   50

    this time of year   51

    the woman they call the town bicycle   52

    slice of pie   53

    midsummer wind   54

    and summer   55

Instructions for Navigating the Labyrinth   59

The CrazyWoman Poems

crazyWoman

worn down to beaten foil
crazyWoman rustles
the wind distracts
magpies with her eyes
quicksilver ballbearings
swivel in sockets

i am down i am down to the bones

stoneground through to chaff
crazyWoman squawks
at birds who flock to steal
bright eyes bright teeth
the once bright hair
to weave into their nests

i am down i am down to the bones

unbuttoned to the bone
crazyWoman swings
by the heels her
meathook gathering
fold and flank glints
mica in pumiced shin

i am down i am down to the bones
i am down to the bones at last

the earth my body this tree

oh what will clot the blood
pelting like darkfruit
the jointure of branches
my thighs windfalls
plumrotten between
the roots of toes

nothing but a baby a baby
the peeled white
head of blue-veined baby
to plug up the bole
for a time for a time

oh what will mute the sound
of an old womb blowing
in high wind rattle
of empty seeds
in dried pods

nothing but the earth the earth
the dark earth's membranes
to shore me up and shoot me out
greencheeked eyes flowering
for a time for a time

with words my tentpegs

it is a world of snow billowing from the sky
wet sheets flapping on a washing line
it is a world of snow and writing
about snow that has fallen all night
in harsh flurries the sound of paper
tearing   your eyes this morning as you lie
beneath banked sheets are full of snow
unshed there is snow in the air
under your lids upon this page it falls
gently not like the damned who
also fall
all night the wind has tried to launch
this flapping house stands upright   still
but only just as long as i
can pinion it to this blank page
with words my tentpegs this poem is one long
guyrope pulled taut across a world of snow
shored up against pale shins   a bird
falls slowly earthwards wings
beat paperthin against the season's
frenzy the snow has reached my arms
flung outward on a cross of climate
and blasphemy   it is a world
of snow and writing about snow i write
through the night and the morning
of the night the morning your eyes
swollen like snowclouds   but i
i still cannot unwind the wind this
blank page swallows my hand like a glove out
in the naked garden snow ruffs the lady's neck
settles in her cold mouth gluts

that flapping tongue who is left now
to tell how the house gave a sudden

                                      jerk
and flew away into a world of snow
tentpegs trailing the wind
guyrope sheds

              words

                    like

                         to r n

                                 p a p e   r

fat lady suites

one-eyed annie walks through the park must
be tha sun cause tha flowers an tha drunksre
out calling hey annie here pusspuss   puss
this is the world my body and i am in it
soft as butter spread as bread smacking
my tulips an dandling my loins oh dry up an
blow youse tha only bulbs not blooming here

one-eyed annie steams the shade braids
plump hair in trellises spits the dust she
says to show her nonevermind   and to make
perhaps flowers grow plucks seeds from her
teeth   tongues us warm in sweetdeep
hair hangs wisteria from the slats between
time   once upon when we was slaves ago

annie cocks an eye blinks twice asks madam
for her wages in advance account of her son
nogoodBoy in jail again   but you still owe
me from last time madam shakes her head
and paysup paysup paysup   nogoodBoy
asks madam for bus money i've no change
at all she says that's alright madam that's ok

i can break you a twenty easy   one-eyed
annie skims the soup steals jars of butter
and jam waters the wine sours the milk
plucks ribbons lace from secret drawers
sucks the yolks out of eggs hawks phlegm
in the wells madam pretends not to notice
that madam she notices every lil ting

crazyWoman loses a button

she has lost the button
that pinned her together like upholstery
to an old armchair she has lost the
button button who's got the button?

must be somewhere in this house
she thinks i had it at my fingertips
thimbleready
only yesterday why
it can't be gone already

and she searches through ribvaulted
chambers calling button button
who's got the . . . rummages
stacks of mattresses fat down
quilts but finds only
for her pains a pea
wherever can it be?

opens a cupboard flung
with dresses brocaded in edible colours
raspberry tangerine pimento and
sage   a shuffle of capsized shoes
one highstepping crystal
slipper the other
like the button
absent

button button . . . the underwear drawer
hisses silk spite stockings
nestle like baby snakes breathe
feet and the smell of feet
oyster-coloured panties hint at
satin interiors, frayed
lace, no button

who's got the button?

she rifles her handbag fingers
loose change loose keys loose
knucklebones, a white handkerchief
three drops of blood, scrawled lines
this is just to say
i will be back a hundred years
from today a vial of perfume
a fountainpen two tampons and
the handmirror (years ago she fell in
and drowned) also
a soft red purse of polished leather
containing perhaps the elusive
button

getting warmer?
burning up!

what's in the purse what's in this last
bluebeard's chamber she picks through
banknotes creditcards a handful
of magic beans, what's to be found
    in the purse in the handbag
    in the drawer in the cupboard
    in the room in the house

button but . . .

            . . . the button of course
            and screws it in
            her own un
            buttoned navel

                    •

a fine grammar of bones

this country was long ago she
remembers a crookwalled town wintersoup
sliced with rutted vegetables there
were no signposts to this town it began
in the margins of a blank page peeled
open to a scroll and when it snowed
she said the world opened into silence
between letters snow falling like words
and the white spaces between words
in another country her daughter
brushes her hair twists tortoiseshell
combs through coils she was dying the sun
shone through her skin to a fine
grammar of bones strummed that pale
ribcage chanted the pious liturgy
of her spine i was queen her bones
rattled in her skin and she died
turning to parchment like the town
where she was born where she was young
was queen was beautiful tamed wild
rubies to her knucklebones fell
ill of language began to die

burning bush

how to preserve her oil lamp packed
upright   dryiced between
grapeskin thighs and she smiles
like a papercut smiles
and smiles and smiles and smiles all
the livelong day one

day she will burn
from the inside out, herself
out, fine streamers of vein
will catch fire inflame
the dry courses of hotwired blood
and tendergreen leaves of organs in bud
strung on that skeleton tree the whole
contagion of bone and bark
gutted, what
a blaze that will be

we will bring our raw fish
to her scouring flame
we will bring our raw hands
to her braziered ribs
and eat from sweet fire
dark roe drenched in oil

a short growing season

who would have thought
the old earth to have
had so much blood how
it gushes congealed

between leaves thick
salty what are we to
do with these tomatoes
first one wells

something fat and hot
grows between us of
us but when it unrolls
you aren't there not

gone just absent so i
eat it that hot mouth
against mine in mine
devoured by mine where

was yours there was
a smell that day like
genesis   they lay
in the dark beheaded

    who would have
thought the earth to
have had so much blood
or what was between us

to be so hungry

crazyWoman remembers water

water remembers old paths has
perfect memory floods its banks
to recall old sluices
i have forgotten everything
but the tides of my body   how

they were pulled from me
by the moon that fattened
each month in the night
of my shuttered thighs how
i peeled in segments at fullquarter

water finds in the body its own
congruence scaling the insides
like a kettle remembers past levels
as signs as letters as words as the words
that remember my past   how

they hissed in the ribbed mahogany
of my mouth words
seasoned in timber passing
like grapes into wine how
they soured to vinegar in time

know then that water would rather freeze
or burn than die know then that water
cannot die the past is unchangeable
words are indestructible memory
too if there is only someone left

to remember there is not much in this
world that can die only the body
hungry for worms and the
small words that remembered me
as i lay as i lay dying as i died

Palm of the Hand Stories

The schoolteacher his wife their dog and the chicken

Nobody loved the schoolteacher not his wife, their children, his dog. But love as he often reminded them is dispensable, respect now, respect was the very air that he breathed. And everyone respected the schoolteacher, the schoolchildren, his wife, their children, his dog why even the chickens in the yard seemed to lower their goggleyes as he passed them beating vigorously the index finger of his right hand in time to the flight of the valkyries that played always, stuck record in his head. And the schoolteacher loved nobody except Wagner who was dead and Isolde who never existed. What is more the schoolteacher respected nobody either so his life if only he knew it foundered daily on analogy.
One day the schoolteacher's dog lost his head and followed his heart, killing in the process a chicken.
Well.
The schoolteacher was so angry he came home so angry so angry the air thickened and congealed with his anger. His wife cowered behind the stove, his children ran and hid beneath their bed, he took the dead chicken and tied it to the dog's collar.
There.
Now the schoolteacher's poor dog had to walk about in the august heat with that dead festering chicken tied by the feet to his collar. The air turned black and glistening with the wings of flies the air grew rancid about that poor dog who ran and ran to get away from the smell and the heat and the flies. But wherever he ran the mess of rotting chicken followed him.
That'll teach him, said the teacher.
And it did too, never ever in all the remaining miserable years of its existence did the schoolteacher's dog so much as glance at another chicken. One day the schoolteacher was returning home late at night from who knows where his wife was careful

never to ask where he went at these times she knew he would tell her the truth.

And the roads were laminated with ice and the dead wintertrees seemed to sprout horns like a company of valkyries as he rode and hummed and plotted the infliction of pain and beat with the index finger of his right hand on the steering wheel as he skidded and braked for a dark form as he crushed the car and killed the animal as he rode and hummed and plotted and beat and skidded and braked and crushed and killed as he flew through the windshield at 120 kilometres per hour braining in the process himself.

The schoolteacher sits on the porch in tepid sunlight rocking himself gently. All the archery and thrust of his mind have been refined by the glass of the windshield to this: this rocking movement in a gentle wind at the beginning of the start of spring.

This.

The schoolteacher sits on the porch and rocks himself gently. The air about him glistens with wings with the glance of light on wings, the air about him thrums to high voltage with the wings of flies that gather to light on the carcass of the dog that he killed in the night. The schoolteacher's dog that the schoolteacher's wife has tied to his ankle to teach him a lesson. Now.

The schoolteacher's wife, the schoolteacher's children can shrug off the pronouns that have worn them thin all their lives. Now the schoolteacher's wife, his children can glide into their own names caressive as bareflesh and seersucker after the long months of winter.

Their names their names, I would tell you their names (I have forgotten their names).

My mother's heart My mother's bitter heart

I am giving my mother a new heart. I dream I am a heart
surgeon performing an openheart transplant on my mother no
one else can save her. There is her old heart in the draining cup
neatly dissected into five pieces one for each of us children and
here in my hands is the new heart plump as a dumpling light as
a soufflé with a sticker that reads *guaranteed up to minus twentyfive*
degrees. As I hold the heart tenderly in my hands it breaks into
song, an old lullaby

      mine kind, mine trayst, dee foorst a-vek
      zay zy a dogter a goo-ter
      dich bate mit treh-ren un mitshrek
      dine try-ye lee-be mut-ter
      dee foorst mine kind, mine ain-tzig kind
      a-rib-ber vy-te yah-men
      ach kum a-heen nor frish ge-zund
      un nit far-gessdine ma-men
      yoh! foor ge-zund un koom mit glik
      zay yay-deh voch a bree-vel shik
      dine ma-mes hertz dine ma-mes bit-ter hertz
      mine kind der-kvik

I recognize the tune it was a song my mother's mother had
often sung to me as a child in the only language that she knew,
a breevele der mamen, a letter to mother

      my child, my comfort you're going away
      see that you remain a good daughter
      with tears and with anguish begs
      your devoted loving mother
      you're going away my only child
      across distant seas
      may you get there in good health
      and don't forget your mother

yes! farewell and get there safely
see that you write a letter once a week
and refresh your mother's heart
your mother's bitter heart
my child

The heart in my hands was just starting in on the refrain a
bree-ve-le der ma-a-men when I packed it deftly in ice and
filed it in the freezer. Don't-for-get-your-moth-er rang the
phone as I woke with salt on my cheeks.

listen I don't have time for chitchat I'm on my way to play
rummy with the girls have you got a date for tonight look I
should rot in hell if I so much as begin to interfere again but
Sadie says there's this boy going free and to be honest that's
what you are and I said to her why should two people be
lonely if four can be happy?
four?
you. me. him. Sadie.
aah
(aah)
all you need to do is make a phone call it's not like I'm pushing
you it's just that a mother doesn't like to die leaving the last of
her children alone in the world . . .

The thing was she was dying so I made the call.

hello
hi this is well you don't really know me but i'm a friend of
Sadie's well not really a friend my mother's the friend actually
and she said you would be expecting my call well i don't usually
do this but you have to understand my mother my mother

He was nice actually. Not Bogey meets Bergman nice not here's lookin' at you kid and damn the torpedoes nice not even frankly Scarlett nice but an ok guy nevertheless with a nice line in chair pulling out, door holding, parcel carrying and no obvious warwounds. We went to a movie we went out for coffee we went to bed. And it was all all very nice. Not come from the root of your spine nice not did you feel the earth move nice not my goodness hard again nice but an overall ok experience with some non-deductible extras like handholding, earblowing, lipsmacking. And he didn't scour himself off afterwards lathering away in my shower out out damn spot didn't even rinse his mouth gargling *to all the girls I've loved before* before spitting succinctly. Nice.

So I invited him to dinner the next week making four people happy with one luminous gesture.

listen, my mother said on the phone, listen I should drop dead for interfering but a man likes to eat it's not enough this fancyshmancy food that looks like it's been painted onto the plate a man's got to eat Sadie says stuffed derma so I took the liberty you should forgive an old woman her last wish of running up a batch didn't take hardly a day and a half which I will deliver with your approval of course as soon as the damn taxi I called half an hour ago he should grow onions in his belly arrives

The thing is she was dying so I replaced the two delicate wafers of sole that I had coaxed from the corner fishmonger only yesterday in the freezer and went out to buy the wine something red and fullbodied to go with motherlove and stuffed derma.

When I came back the police were at my door shuffling their
turnip feet and twisting their hats in their hams and begging to
inform me that they were sorry to announce that there had
been an accident. Corner fifth and main, an old lady and a
taxidriver, stuffed derma everywhere.
Well there goes my entrée I thought.

So I took her heart out of the freezer and defrosted it in half an
hour by running hot water in the sink and rubbed it with garlic
and basil and ground pepper and coarse salt and stuck it with
cloves and orangesticks to sweeten the bitterness and by three
o'clock it was basting in a gravy refulgent with redwine and
bayleaves and at eight o'clock he arrived I took his coat and we
sat down to refresh ourselves on french bread and green salad
and my mother's heart my mother's bitter heart.

Take one of mine said Olivia

Take one of mine said Olivia when I found I was all out of
cigarettes so I did and inhaled deeply filling my lungs like
parachutes with the fragrant smoke and leaned back to look at
her. She was big with story, brought to full term by some
breathless tale or other that she had called me forth to deliver
across the starched white cloth of the corner table at
Halfmoon Café where we met every few months or so to drink
blackcurrant tea and eat the cinammon rolls that nowhere else
in the city grew so sticky and lick our fingers and remind
ourselves of other lives and other loves but briefly briskly
without sentiment or nostalgia Olivia can tolerate sugar only in
her tea. It is difficult to remain friends with old lovers and we
are certainly not friends we are I was going to say confidantes
but that implies familiarity and all that it breeds, no we are
witnesses that is the word that most deftly describes the brief
windows into eachothers lives that we permit ourselves before
awkwardly fumbling down the shutters.
No I am wrong, Olivia is never awkward.
Thank you, no, she tells the waitress graciously when she
brings us the usual plate of sticky buns, not today. The
morning sickness will not permit me you see and her peculiar
sense of comradeship will not permit her at this delicate time,
we are, we have always been sisters beneath the skin.
Now she takes her own elegant time carefully measuring out
one spoonful of honey to stir into the plush tea, the most
important part of the story is the beginning.

This story (she begins) has a strong punchline but it is not a
joke promise me you will not think it a joke. It is not a joke, an
anecdote, a parable. It is true I was there or else it is not true
but I was there remember that (she frowns and I promise to

take into account the ungainly punchline of this story how she hates surprises which is odd perhaps considering her vocation although taking all things into account she is an excellent midwife).

I was up north on that flying doctor program I told you about (one eyebrow ironically cocked since she knows she has told me no such thing) past Churchill at one of the northern reserves the clinics up there are terribly basic no facilities for special deliveries no doctors no sober ones at any rate no blankets even often the women bring their own sheets in have the baby then gather up linen and baby and body and leave well it was the full moon shift don't ever let anyone tell you differently the babies come out with the moon so they do sure as apples we had two mothers in there bearing down and yelling and swearing I said look you should have said that to him nine months ago now's not the time push mamma push the older woman was going licketysplit   fortyeight years with eight children and what looked like twins to grow on but the other woman was only sixteen with a cervix like a sardine can no way we were going to crank the kid out alive I knew that Hannah Goodhands knew that take a deep breath and push she cried my little one pushpushpush and she did too for a long time until the baby slid out stillborn on the table and flopped to death in my hands then at last it was quiet in the birthing room the older woman lay quiet her two babies lay quiet on her stomach Hannah Goodhands took the dead baby from me and left the room quietly quietly and the mother we still call them mothers even with no baby to show for it how else to mourn the little dead ones the mother lay quiet and it was quiet for a long long time (it was quiet for a long long time so quiet I heard the tea curl slowly down her throat) and then she said it (quiet quiet)

26

What did she say?
That thing I told you the punchline, the older woman with the
twins turned to the kid and said
(quiet quiet)
What did she say?

Take one of mine she said.

Presently the waitress came to bring us more hot water and I
handed my empty cup to Olivia who swirled the tealeaves
round before emptying them on my saucer, small things she
said the loss of small things, nothing precious this time, just
small things lost, misplaced. We smiled I am always losing
small things and talked some more at ease because it was
afterwards as it had been so many times between us,
afterwards, and rose to leave together at ease and part again, at
ease this time for good. And because she knew I had misplaced
my cigarettes again (again) before she left she flipped me hers.

Something I've been meaning

The nightwatchman had a name a face that nobody could
remember so they called him Bombardier which was the slogan
scrawled on the back of his secondhand parka in soiled red
stitching. Bombardier who was a salt dried man with a heart
like a wringer in the thin washingboard of his chest had never
before been given a nickname, it was the best job he'd ever
had. Nights at the store locked into the empty rooms, the
electrical outlets humming his old bones dry he'd fix himself an
egg salad and sweet pickle sandwich from the grill and settle
down in the audio department to watch the evening news on
the store's giant television screen. Afterwards he'd take a walk
through the department store solemn and selfconscious, hands
clasped behind his back like a businessman like an owner.
Taking stock.
It was on one of these inventories that he fell in love.
It began in the mirror. She was very beautiful, seamless and
rare the colours on her face precise as enamel her skull a
perfect higharched egg. She was very beautiful the mirror was
undoubtedly a true and fitting habitation and as he stepped
forward to join her there he had such a vision of grace that his
heart turned sun. Light and warmth flooded his bones and beat
gold. He stretched out hesitantly a hand to touch and she flew
apart, the mirror dimmed. That is when he fell in love his body
jarring open and shut a door swung loose on a rusty hinge, he
fell in love with the upthrust of her the way she fell apart in
segments at his feet.
Alchemy is not a word we use nowadays let us speak rather of
mechanics how he gathered her up and put her together again
till she stood perfect as parody before him, his obscure and
most gracious object of desire. He dressed her in the finest
underclothes the lingerie department could offer choosing the

throbbing colours of midnight and negotiating all manner of clips and clasps with a dexterity born of fantasy, thin fingers stroking satin soft as tongue.

He loved her truly deeply madly she was his precious honey baby he was crazy for her nuts about her she was his only. When the day's shoppers had left and the assistants closed down the tills for the night, the store in all its hushed reverie was his to command and she also was his. Then she would place her perfect mouth on his thin lips slide her tongue down the back of his throat to the soles of his feet wrap her hairless thighs about his waist and rock him in the catscradle of her inscrutable body until morning. The ways of her desire were precarious and wayward he was trackless in her arms taking direction only from the beating of her pulse. In the cracked light of dawn he would stagger home and sleep until dusk, he was always hungry.

She never spoke except in cipher. Once she said, do you see that mirror, yes? Well it doesn't see you.

Just so.

She had taken lately to roaming the store in the early evening gathering the fetishes of her delight for his delectation, a feather boa a pair of high-buttoned gloves a bowler hat, she would greet him in stilettoes her body tilted awkwardly in space launched recklessly against gravity and desire her feet sternly bound. Do you see that mirror?

He lived in fear for her safety for she was growing restless he knew, insatiable in her dark storeroom of mirrors, hungry for eyes other than his own to own her. Meanwhile she stalked the perfume counters spraying scent on all her pressure points, preening her wigs to a frenzy.

One day so great was his fear his love that he wrote her a letter.

there is something I've been meaning to say sometime
between the day you kissed me and turned toad and
the day I kissed you and fell asleep for a hundred years
there is something I must tell you I nearly did last
night you were all yellow and butter in my mouth I
couldn't speak

there is something I've been meaning to say

He stuck a postage stamp tenderly on the righthand corner, a
kiss, and sent the letter off but before she could receive it,
something happened.
It ended in the mirror. Before he could get to her she had fallen
in and drowned all that remained was an arrangement of
nipples and eyes, delicate watermarks welling slowly to the
surface.
The nightwatchman has a name a face that nobody can
remember they have even forgotten his nickname. He is a man
who looks in mirrors and waits for a letter, that is all. Not
much to remember a man by, this looking this waiting. In fact
he is slowly beginning to disappear, piece by piece the
nightwatchman is becoming invisible. First the slogan on his
parka began to unravel then his fine webbed fingertips the
drawstring lips and now it is his skin that is unravelling in
intricate yarn, soon not even bones thrifty as knitting needles
will be able to gather him together again, not even bones.
Would it comfort him to know that she has received his letter
that she has understood it that she has already heard what he
has been trying to say? Would it comfort him to know that
already she has sent a reply of her own? It comes down to this
wherever he walks in the darkened store the mirrors track him
with their gaze, the mirrors remember, it is the mirrors who
watch as he turns to glass before their eyes.

A little bird dreamed Maya

A little bird, dreamed Maya in the moments before she awoke and found him gone. Feathers fell silently through the darkness behind her eyes there was an indrawn breath on the mirror the smell of his shaving lotion lingered the air. Outside darkness gathered at the corners, oh I'll be late she thought and struggled out of the hollow of his absent body. Downstairs on the fridge he had pinned a note, meet me at André's usual time. It was their anniversary, one year to the day since the day they had stood together at low watermark cold gulls, bereft and tideless. In the corner of the note, a smudg fingerprint.

She dresses herself with care from the inside out smoothing white satin against the grain of skin. A year of birds, she thinks fleetingly, settling a pearl in the hollow of throat. He had turned to her then, they did not touch she had turned to him he turned they do not touch.

It is already dark when she leaves the house stars string the sky to tinsel a halfmoon carousels the night. Oh my, she looks at her watch, I'm sure to be late.

The traffic is sluggish and wayward ahead beyond the bridge she thinks she catches sight of his car aah well he'll have to wait she thinks, I've waited too.

He had bent that day and lifted from the sand at her feet a feather. Here he said.

At last the blockage is removed the road sluices open cars corpuscle their way to the city. It must have been an accident Maya thinks averting her eyes from a twist of wreckage she catches a glimpse of blood on the white of a shirt and the face above the shirt is white also.

To her surprise he is not there when she arrives but André makes her comfortable in the corner booth with the mirrors, their table. In the last year they have become collectors, pressing words between pages, laying endearments behind glass, cataloguing the valuables: their song their place their table. André brings her a scotch and places a dry sherry at the other setting. Their drinks.

Still he does not come Maya crumbles a breadstick orders another scotch. She blows smoke in the mirror play it again Sam from the corner of her mouth, play it right.

Here he said. They do not touch.

It is late she has been stood up. She stands up, the mirror wavers as she walks to the door. André smoothes her into her coat punctilious, will madam be all right? Madam will.

It is late she drives toward the bridge, perhaps he is dead she thinks vengefully, he better be.

It is late she drives toward the bridge slowing down to pass the car twisted into wreckage something flickers she recognizes the car her heart yolks open, he is dead.

Maya runs through the night shedding satin her hair snags the moon she slips on a star it takes forever to reach his car. What is so sad is the broken heel of her shoe the run in her stocking what is so sad is the pearl about her throat can never be a kiss it takes forever to reach his car. If this were a poem it would go

Maya runs through the night Maya
runs through the night Maya runs
through the night Maya runs through
the night Maya runs through the
night Maya runs through the night

It is the night that runs through Maya in the end it is the night
floods membranes like ink she is all squid now and black her
heart in the shape of an owl swoops the sky a moon in its claw.

It takes forever to reach. She reaches. His car.

Maya sees something sprawled across the seat a face white
above the bloodspattered white of a shirt. They do not touch.

How the dead remember us! Maya stares into her own face
white above white Maya stares. So he is alive she thinks, after
all.

The eyes of the woman in the car are glazed but Maya thinks
she sees the feathers that fall silently in the darkness behind
them in the moments before they open Maya dreams of a little
bird and wakes up dead to find him gone again.

Anyplace but here

That Hoosier woman runs through the town on the day of the
fires calling here puss here pusspusspuss. Her hair a wild
distraction she has just come off the lunch hour shift at the
soup and sandwich kitchen on main now she runs calling, her
skirts gusting onions and the smell of lunchmeat.
Well everyone was running that day couldn't blame them down
main street over the railway tracks to the trailerpark through
the hospital parking lot everyone was running. Still she did not
go unnoticed, it was Elvira Keeler staunch at her post in the
bank who told later how she caught the heel of her slingback
in a grating and how she fell headlong and how she scrambled
up palms bleeding and ran on barefoot and calling. Well
everyone was calling that day, mothers to children husbands to
wives farmers to cattle, there was a ferocious calling of voices
and counting of heads that day. The day that came to be called
the Day.
Four seasons on the prairies, winter's coming, winter's
here, winter's over, nearly winter. Seems it was only
yesterday old man Noordenbos is fond of adding sipping tea
through the sugar cube in his front teeth, seems it was only
yesterday.
Rumour has it that the sky on the day of the fire passed
overhead like the belly of a fat white shark, underneath people
ran in circles calling. There is a moment in the intransigent life
of towns between the waters of the last snowfall and the waters
of the first springfall when there is no water none at all. That is
the moment when the earth gapes open and the fires come
through. Who was it said that?
Could have been Pastor Dyck, a minister and embalmer of
philosophic bent on this day he comes into his own the whole
town speaks afterwards of how he shucked his black coat for a

parka and turned firefighter with the farmers on the edges of
the town. Some say he showed character the true spirit of the
prairies where nothing grows but rocks and the secret is to
adapt. Others call him a coward fighting the fire seen is
nothing they say to the fires unseen, the sin is to adapt. But
from his vantage point on the edge of the town the pastor is in
time to see that Hoosier woman stumble past his church
leaving red palmprints on a doorpost, the pastor is startled.
Thing is it's just a highstreet-hospital-threechurch kind of place
same as anywhere else, thing is t'ain't anyplace but here.
As for Mandy Strand of Strand's Cash 'n Carry to hear her tell
it she was in such a state from herding up her firestruck
children she clear lost her mind to the anxiety of the moment
and hoisted a bag of Florida oranges into the backseat of her
starwagon along with the youngest boy. Which gave them
something to do at least as they idled on high ground sucking
fruit and watching the flames peel orange watching the men
plough up the highstreet for a fire-line watching that Hoosier
woman run down the railway tracks to the trailerpark
screaming like a whistle.
The trailerpark is on the other side of the railway tracks the
wrong side. Living in the trailerpark is of necessity being
intimate with your neighbour's garbage. Also what they are
cooking for dinner what time their husbands tack home from
the motor hotel pub and poolroom whether their kids push
drugs or steal hockey cards and when they choose to wash
their cars. Living in the trailerpark is an exercise in
secondhand emotions, dry and flammable. Some say the fire
started in the trailerpark some say the trailerpark simply
combusted with the pent up rhythm of indrawn breaths, at all
events it was the trailerpark that went up first bonewhistledust
dry on the edges of the prairie quick as a wink a flash a flick of
the pulse.

I wasn't there but this is what they say, they say she paused a moment before stepping into her house her flaming house all over the town it seems they heard her call here puss here pusspusspuss.

After the fire had eaten the Hoosier woman it belched and slowed some and by the end of the day it was just a thin wisp of smoke fanning the wings of the prairie grass and they all went home the women counting heads and calling still the men smelling of smoke in the mesh of their bodies even the pastor dropped his sack and turned reluctant eyes to his steeple.

As for the cat I guess you know there never was one or if there was it died the week before. Of old age, they say.

Tailored Desires

girl in a yellow dress

                              look!
i am all in yellow for once decked
in lemon light and ochre shadow
buttercup pumpkin daffodil
citrine with
tigereyes opal hair my
fingernails ten moonstones
at full quarter   my bush
a minor sun

long ago i read if a man glances
for only one second at a girl
in a yellow dress the electrons
in his eyes vibrate
fivehundredquadrillion
times registering
more oscillations in that
one
     second
than all the waves that ever beat
on all the shores that have ever been washed
into all the oceans in ten million
years think of that

and dear
because a second is
all i get from you most
days
    one
second measured carefully care
less one grain
of sand falling
between the halves of an hour
glass one
cone of light dropping
between lid and lash
it pleases me to think
of all those electrons pounding
with all the waves
on all the shores
of all the oceans
that ever were it pleases
me to make you throb

a taste for butter

my childhood was
mostly food
and the words of a song
about food   row
row row your boat
gently down the stream
mer-rilymer-rilymer-rilymer
rily-life-is
            i thought it was
butter-dreams my slow
child's mind dredging
images of streams churning
past trees hung with fruit
butterbright in thick leaves

and we rowed bending
over the boatsedge dipped
popcorn thumbs in the salted tide
until the boat ran aground
on an island
called never-never
again land
            there grew
all the melodious fruits
of childhood: cherryjellyberries
(goose-blue-rasp-and-straw   take
your pick)
hotdogsodas
pizzashakes
chilisundaes

what is there in childhood
but toeatoeatoeateateat
or be eaten? everything
was cut and gulp then
fingers squirming in honeyjars
hands bunched tight with nuts
mouths running jam and pumpkin
and warm yellow yolk chins
coated with peachjuice

and when all the food
was gone the gingerbread
houses and chocolate
soldiers and stolen apples
were all all eaten and gone
why then we sat down to eat
ourselves up again
sucking pale toes
like boiled sweets
streamers of wet hair
liquorice-dark
and mouths like cut
plums

years since i ran aground
that attic island bobbing mer-
rilymerrily in the buttery stream
nowadays i rarely eat it is not
the fashion but sometimes
i resonate to a tuning fork
with the taste of butter

redDress

redDress hangs in the cupboard
where magic things happen to
beautiful skins worn by
bad women she twitches until
midnight strokes then climbs
off the crucifix of her wire
hanger and pleasures in the
bare moonlight herself peels
nude in segments like ripe
fruit herself a sleeve here
a rain of gold buttons and then
all the fiddling plumage
her coy skirts
    opening
           out like
a courtesan's fan like
a handful of slander like
a peacock's tail redDress
folds back into the cupboard
as the first spill of dawn
unrolls the sky a bolt of
silk cloth impales herself
    still
        twitching
on the hanger
of her tailored desire

i love a red dress just
one shade brighter than
ripetorotten raspberries when
you cut open the pieflap and
vividjuice steams through
crust reminds us of
mortal things the vagaries
of flesh the way the blood
          roils
                    just
below the surface hisses
at the first brutality of
the serving knife seeps
through to stain pale
crusts of flesh

insideout on the washing line beside
a flock of white underwear a pair
of starched black crows watching
her dark reflection wrack and writhe
in pegged sunlight   redDress
decides enough is enough is
   sufficient
            plots
selfdestruction threads
herself through the taut
running noose dies
as she lived in high
   dudgeon
                sliding
graciously off the line and
out of this life transformed
at the moment of her waning
shedding the old skin glib
as a zipper
                look!
at the lady on the flying trapeze how
she highwires the breeze there are
soapsuds in her toes a clothespeg
on her nose and nothing between
but her unbaked flesh pale
and piecrust tender

This Time of Year

these thirsty flowers

these thirsty flowers
gulp down all of
yesterday's sunlight
grow yellow and fat
at the glut drain
the afternoon pale display
much the same etiquette
when captured in bottles
set to blaze
at dim interiors
where they dredge
at their waters
through stalks like straws

the vase is half empty
that yesterday was full
still they laplaplaplap
green tongues trough
night's waters

i mean coyotes

white fields lap
the invisible seam
of white sky, bones
fan, a deck of cards
four black-aced hooves
one eye cocked bloody
as the ace of diamonds
the other closed

what violence was this
slow death between blunt teeth
beneath a cabbagepeel moon those
soft ribs snouted open the heart
neatly cored gulped down

we strode our ski-doos, shot
out of there down humpbacked roads
past sleeping owls, a disused quarry
a herd of cows a lake a valley
thrumming with electricity

and the railway tracks rattled
to keep pace the wind
opened red flags in our cheeks
as our machines carried us over
the horizon where a calf lay
gutted in the snow in an empty
field or sky dragged there
last night by wolves i mean
coyotes.

this time of year

dry days pulled taut
between the last snowfall
and the sudden whoosh of spring
opening out like a green umbrella
the sun come home to roost singing
ain't nothing gonna burn now

but before between
when the brown earth's thin skin
crackles like potroast the trees
kindling with each rasp
of wind dead branches
tossed together like shank
bones   the whole ashen prairie
coffined to a tinderbox
only needs a passing match
a stray thought a wicked wish
to set the whole to blazes this

is a time of dark glasses sore throats
and waiting
sit behind drawn blinds
talk behind cupped hands of
two years past when the snow
had just melted and the sap
not yet risen and
the fires
started coming through

the woman they call the town bicycle walks home along the dusty road

that crosses the railway tracks to the trailer park one saturday
night with the moon slung low in the sky and her democratic
ass slung similarly low in a pair of jeans that (like the moon her
ass and all of us) have seen better days   i want to put it all in
a story the northern night the woman's haunchy swaybacked
walk the way she stumbles across the tracks to tell in
pumping-iron prose how we had seen her in the texaco diner
off highway #6 sitting alone at a table she drinks diet pepsi
stares into space past the truckers who wolf their 24 hour
breakfasts at 10 in the evening gouging the yellow eyes of fried
eggs they slop coffee into cracked saucers   plastic daisies
plastic bottles of ketchup and ranch dressing the waitress at full
term and the beachboys singing of southern girls and southern
waves you heard it first on your goldenoldie station   she
wasn't smoking although she would have in my story   it
would have been the kind of thing a maverick midwestern
director would have loved starring an actress with bruised lips
her hair an unmade bed suggesting no doubt her natural
habitat   the roar of a semi-trailer at irregular but ironic
intervals and softdrink machines featuring the names of rival
manufacturers   it would have made a scorcher of a play the
kind we have come to expect from wellbred southern
gentlemen carefully contrived flashbacks to a mangled
childhood bare feet and happy incest train whistles in the
background a dead child as subplot   the woman they call the
town bicycle walks home along the dusty road when she
reaches the railway tracks we stop and offer her a lift   no
thanks she says i like to walk

slice of pie

the first rhubarb pie she ever made was good her mother said
look dad is taking his second slice he wouldn't if it wasn't
her father snorted and allowed (fingers jammy) it was the first
thing she'd ever made that looked like a pie at least   everyone
laughed she laughed too pleased at the success of this pie pleased
even at the failure of the others that had earned his good humour
through their defect her husband laughed (mouth full) fed piecrust
to his dogs the kids spilled onto the porch like loose change   aw
rhubarb maw yuck   silting sugar on the tart pink slices that
she had thought perfectly balanced between the sweet shortcrust
of innocence and the sourdough of call it experience for want
of a better word there is a better word (it's guilt) look out
she said feeling the slipstream of air behind her bare neck open
and close with the whirr of tiny wings   here come the mosquitoes
and she gathered up her newest born in one arm and the pie in the
other reflecting that she had made both and only one looked like a
pie so her father wasn't entirely incorrect in his assessment of
her housewifery

midsummer wind

shaken awake like trees by the wind   the world breaks
wind snatches the earth bare as scalp stuffs throats with
grass mouths plugged with hair somewhere a door is latched
unlatched all night swinging loosehinge the day pivots in
its own blown frenzy undone by clouds that flap telephone
lines an old shirt maddens hangs itself from the washing
line a crop of dandelions fall beheaded by night   fall
and cats chasing thei˞ own tails hurtle through swarms of
bees blown off course far from their forsaken queen who
preens herself one last time in an empty hive in a wind
blown field then dies the earth cracks tarpaulin the wind
opens hollowboned wings in the chambers of our ears some
where a door swings o(pen and shut o)pen and the unhinged
day swings open and shuts one last time and it's later
than we think

and summer

we are folding away summer we hang lawnchairs on hooks in dark
barns stow the barbecue away with the smell of last season's
sausages still ripe beneath its hood catch plush globes of
fruit behind glass we are folding summer like the good sheets
in the guest room   against the bias everything gone under
ground now skunks into holes sheets into cupboards hands into
pockets   and summer   summer hangs somewhere in the dark
hooked between dusty garden furniture and an outboard motor
we never use in nine months time you will blunder in searching
for galoshes and release her pierced to the heart but game to
try again one last time or else swinging from her butcher's
hook either way there will be the fatstink of meat to grow on

Instructions for Navigating the Labyrinth

How do you enter the labyrinth?
Turn left turn left turn left.

These are the facts: the embalmed corpses of seven women
their throats slit are found in a sealed basement in a house on
the outskirts of the city by the mistress of the house. Her name
is Annah her husband is away on business he is a travelling
salesman for a company that markets razor blades and stainless
steel kitchen knives. They are found at the noon hour by the
wife who has disobeyed her husband: Annah beware never
enter the basement never never enter the basement.

Seven women! One for every day of the week?

Everything that happens is a clue.

More facts: Annah and her husband have been married for a
full year when she makes her discovery. They live together in
the house with an old family servant called Belia. Tonight is
their wedding anniversary Annah's husband is expected home
at seven they are going out to dinner at an expensive restaurant
in the city. Afterwards, well he is a man of habit, afterwards he
will pitchfork her to the bed with his iron thighs and pour
himself into her creamy interiors, Annah beware never enter
the basement, never never . . .

Annah and her husband have been married for one year and it
has been a good year. He has been a kind husband by her
lights, he likes his coffee strong and his women weak. Annah
buys the best Brazilian roast and grinds it herself adding
chicory and lemon peel at the end. When she went to live with

him in the three storey house on the outskirts of the city that he inherited from his father, he gave Annah the keys to all the rooms.
Except one.

You know the rest.

At some point all analogies break down.

Long ago when Annah first went to live with her husband on the outskirts of the city, he gave her the keys of the house hung from an antique gold chatelaine. This was his wedding gift to her she has worn it about her waist for the last year because she loves her husband and tradition and the luxurious mesh of heavy gold link. There are seven silver keys hanging from her waist and they clink against each other as she walks.
clink clink clink
Annahmylove calls her husband when he hears her chains, my precious girl . . .

clink clink clink

Reader beware never enter the basement never never enter the basement!

Annah's husband, we will call him B, is leaving on a short business trip. Goodbye Annahmylove he kisses her, goodbye goodbye.

Three objects lie in a field it is spring: two stones, a red scarf, a raw carrot.

When her husband leaves, Annah calls Belia and together they take up all the carpets and begin to beat them. Dust flies how it flies, a good thing B is not here, Annah says, his hayfever! Clink go the keys at her waist with each stroke of the carpetbeater, clink clink clink.

Think of it this way: if the scarf were not red, the stones not paired, the carrot not raw, think of the time the place the season . . .

After the carpets she and Belia get busy on the floors, Annah rolls her skirt above her waist so that her legs swing free. They are thick strong legs with tightly bunched muscles, they are B tells her, twining them about his neck, one of her finest attributes. Annah is proud of her legs and the things they can do to B to make him forget his nice judgements his way with language. Belia glances sideways at Annah's legs but does not hitch up her skirts.

It is spring the snows have melted. That was a clue.

One of the things Annah has planned to do on this carbonated day at the year's hinge, the air like soda, leaves fizzing up out of bud, one of the things she must do before celebrating with her husband their first wedding anniversary is to attend to the stuffed animals. Meanwhile she has Belia soak the crystal, polish the silver, handwash the fine bedlinen. Belia works slowly with a great creaking of joints but Annah is flushed with spring cleaning, hectic with spring fever, her hair falls about her neck in damp intimate tendrils and she whistles in her pale new skin, sloughing the old one in mothballs with the winter jackets and woollen blankets. It is spring it is spring the snows have melted it is spring.

The snows have melted the rains have come. Nothing remains
in the gushing fields of last year's snowmen but the
stones-for-eyes, the carrot-nose, the red scarf.

Along with the house and old Belia, the stuffed animals were a
legacy to the young couple from Annah's father-in-law, a
prodigious hunter and taxidermist of some repute.

What is the significance of the scarf being red?
Red is the colour of winter scarves and herrings.

Although Annah hates to think of the small suffering creatures
of this world, the blank-eyed squirrels, numb-winged geese,
rabbits stunned by fear and light, the blood in the footprints of
the snowfox, she is the keeper of the stuffed animals. But still
she avoids their empty eyes even as she brush brush brushes
the gloss of their living deadfur.

Annah has attended to the stuffed animals.

> what is green
> can be hung on the wall
> and whistles?

Annah is bored.

> a herring of course!

When Annah is bored her thoughts cluster like metal filings
about the one thing she has been forbidden to think about.
The basement draws her thoughts at these times like iron, the
basement opens and she falls through the trapdoor skirts
whirling above her head.

a herring of course!
But a herring isn't green . . .

How do you enter the basement?
Walk down three flights, turn left.

but a herring isn't green!
It is if you paint it green . . .

Annahmylove beware never enter the basement never never
enter the basement.

it is if you paint it green!
But a herring doesn't hang on the wall . . .

This is the point where analogy breaks down.

but a herring doesn't hang on the wall!
It does if you nail it to the wall . . .

turn left turn left turn left

it does if you nail it to the wall!
But a herring doesn't whistle . . .

clinkclinkclinkclink

but a herring doesn't whistle!
Okay, so a herring *doesn't* whistle.

Annah stands before the forbidden door the seventh key is in
her hand click she turns the lock, click. Somewhere far
overhead old Belia the maid rummages through dirty laundry

and her own stale desires. Annah opens the door Annah enters
the room. Somewhere far overhead another door opens a
sneeze is heard Annahmylove I'm home atishoo!

what is green, can be hung on the wall . . .

The women have the same glassy look of betrayal in their dead
eyes as they swing on their hooks in the gloom of this last this
forbidden room. Annah thinks of the old man who first owned
the house her father-in-law, the hunter, the preserver.
Annahmylove calls her husband, my precious girl.
Of course.
Annah feels fear uncurl a hedgehog in her belly her heart
sluices open strangely there is nothing of incredulity in her
horror it is all all somehow familiar, appropriate even. Besides
it has happened before. Seven times already.

atishoo atishoo atishoo coming closer

There is a rustle in the dark beside her, a hand pulls her into
the room shuts the door silently, we must hide whispers old
Belia, we must hide from the master. I will save you my
precious she whispers lovingly, but Annah hears the
razorblades in her voice.

These are the facts: the embalmed corpses of eight women
hang in a sealed basement in a three storey house on the
outskirts of the city. Once a woman called Annah lived there
with her husband and an old servant named Belia. No longer.
Only two people live in the big house now and it is rapidly
becoming far too much work for one woman.

How do you leave the labyrinth?

Why not hire another servant, asks B.
Good help is hard to come by my love, replies Annah.

Turn left turn left turn

Photo: Mark Bryer

Méira Cook was born in Johannesburg, South Africa, where she worked as an arts journalist and university lecturer. Her prose and poems have appeared in *Canadian Fiction Magazine, Dandelion, Prairie Fire, Border Crossings* and *Absinthe.* She currently lives and writes in Winnipeg, Manitoba.

Recent Poetry from Turnstone Press

Inscriptions: A Prairie Poetry Anthology
Dennis Cooley, editor

this only home
Dennis Cooley

You Don't Get to Be a Saint
Patrick Friesen

Falling in Place
Patrick O'Connell

standing all the night through
Audrey Poetker